First Friends 1

Activity Book

Susan Iannuzzi

OXFORD

UNIVERSITY PRESS

Level 1 Scope and sequence

Topic	Structure	Vocabulary	Letters and phonics	Numbers	Songs and chants
1 Me	I'm… Hello Bye How are you? I'm fine, thank you. Clap Stand up Sit down Point to	Adam Baz Jig Pat Tess	**Aa** Adam, apple **Bb** Baz, bird		**Lesson 2:** Hello, how are you? **Lesson 3:** Letter song **Lesson 4:** Point to Jig **Lesson 5:** Letter song
2 My classroom	What's this? It's a…	bin board chair door picture table window	**Cc** cat, coat **Dd** date, dog	1–2	**Lesson 3:** Letter song **Lesson 4:** Count one and two **Lesson 5:** Letter song
3 My toys	This is my… This is your…	ball balloon boat car doll robot teddy bear	**Ee** egg, elephant **Ff** fan, fig	3–4	**Lesson 3:** Letter song **Lesson 4:** One, two, three, four **Lesson 5:** Letter song **Lesson 6:** Time for fun
4 My things	How many? Plurals How old are you?	bag book lunch box pencil pencil box rubber water bottle	**Gg** girl, give **Hh** hand, horse	5	**Lesson 2:** How old are you? **Lesson 3:** Letter song **Lesson 4:** Doll and teddy bear **Lesson 5:** Letter song
5 My colours	It's + colour (green).	circle rectangle square triangle blue green orange red yellow	**Ii** iguana, insect **Jj** Jig, jump **Kk** kick, kite	6–7	**Lesson 3:** Letter song **Lesson 4:** Hungry iguana **Lesson 5:** Letter song

Topic	Structure	Vocabulary	Letters and phonics	Numbers	Songs and chants
6 My farm	Is it a…? Is it (red)? Yes, it is. / No, it isn't.	butterfly donkey duck field flower goat sun	**Ll** lemon, lion **Mm** mango, moon **Nn** nose, nut	8–9	**Lesson 3:** Letter song **Lesson 4:** Animal song **Lesson 5:** Letter song
7 My clothes	What colour is it? It's… What colour are they? They're…	jumper shirt shoes shorts skirt socks trousers	**Oo** octopus, ostrich **Pp** Pat, pink **Qq** queen, quiet	10	**Lesson 3:** Letter song **Lesson 4:** Ten birds, here with me **Lesson 5:** Letter song
8 My body	I've got…	arms ears eyes feet fingers head legs	**Rr** rabbit, run **Ss** seesaw, sing **Tt** Tess, toes		**Lesson 3:** Letter song **Lesson 4:** I've got ten fingers **Lesson 5:** Letter song
9 My family	He / She is… They are…	baby brother dad grandma grandpa mum sister	**Uu** umbrella, up **Vv** van, volcano **Ww** walk, water		**Lesson 3:** Letter song **Lesson 4:** Come and meet my family **Lesson 5:** Letter song
10 My food	I like… / I don't like…	banana biscuit carrot orange sandwich sweet tomato	**Xx** box, fox **Yy** yo-yo, yogurt **Zz** zebra, zero		**Lesson 3:** Letter song **Lesson 4:** Alphabet song **Lesson 5:** Letter song

1 Me

1 Match and say.

1 Find and circle.

2 Draw and colour.

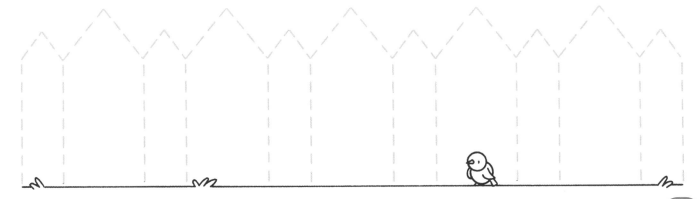

1 Trace and write.

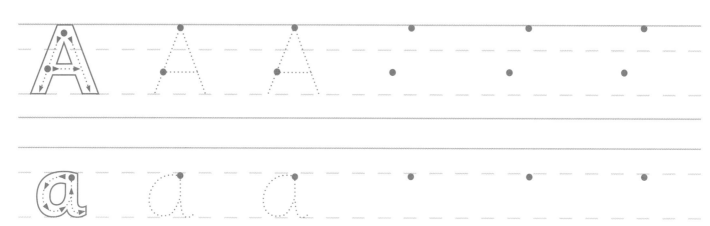

2 Trace and say. Colour.

Adam

apple

1 Draw and match.

Tess •▸

Baz

Jig

Pat

1 Trace and write.

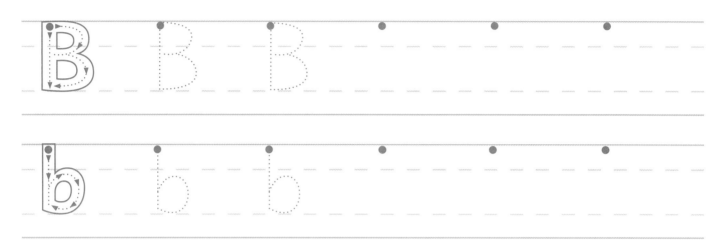

2 Trace and say. Colour.

Baz

bird

1 Match and say.

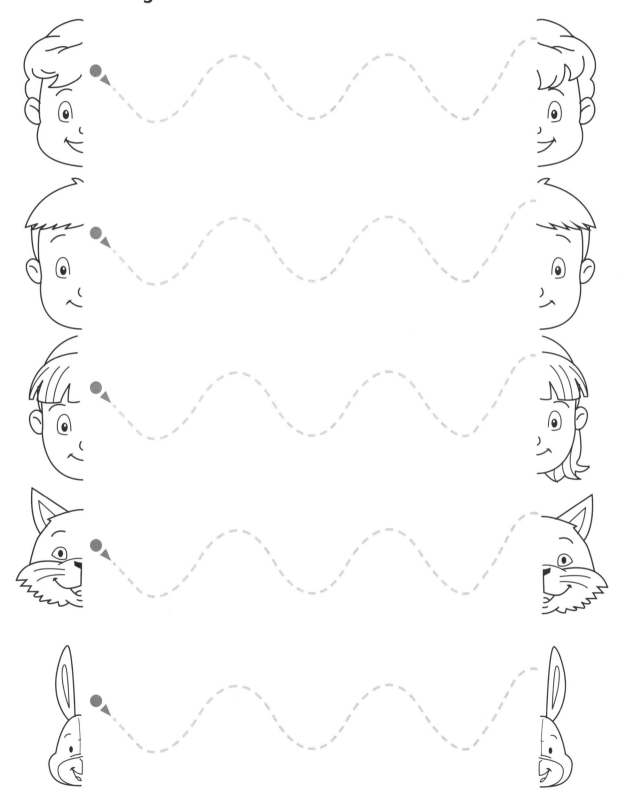

1 Find and circle.

a	b	a	b	b
b	a	a	b	a
A	B	B	B	A
B	B	A	A	A

2 Match and colour.

A   a   B   b

2 My classroom

1 Match and say.

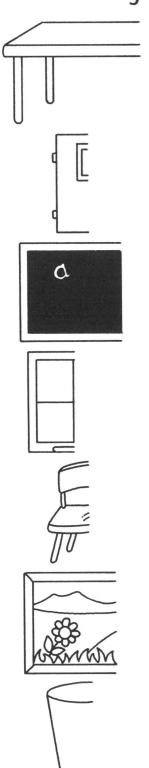
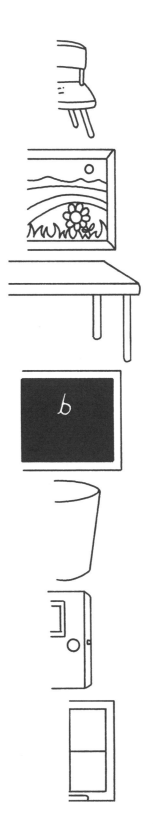

1 Draw and say.

2 Draw and colour.

1 Trace and write.

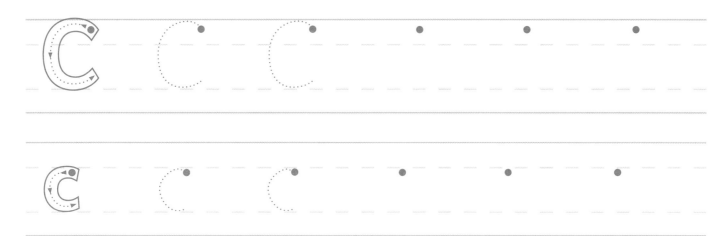

2 Trace and say. Colour.

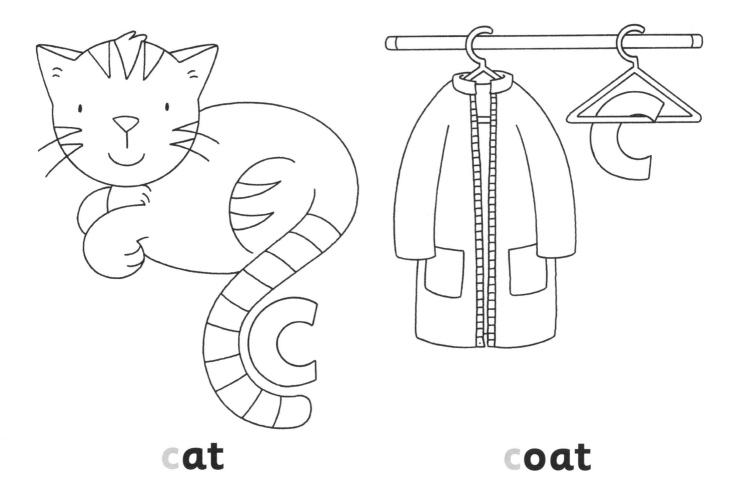

cat   coat

1 Count and circle.

2 Trace and write.

1 Trace and write.

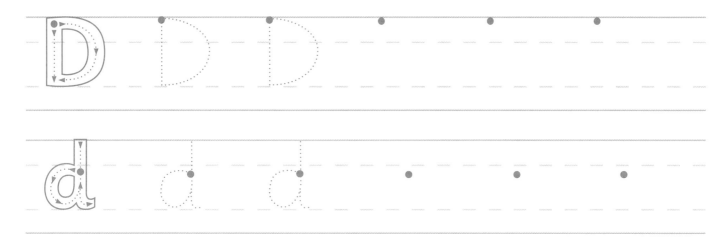

2 Trace and say. Colour.

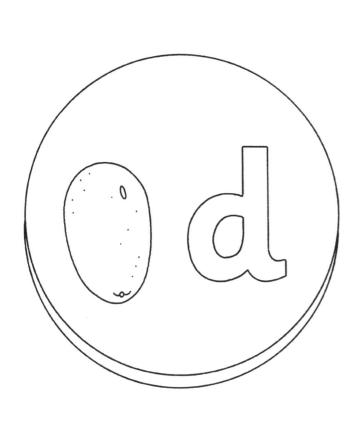

date

dog

1 Colour the letters **C** and **c**.

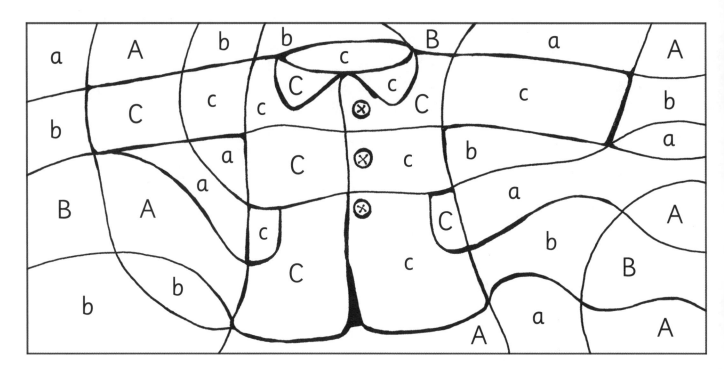

2 Colour the **D** and **d** dates.

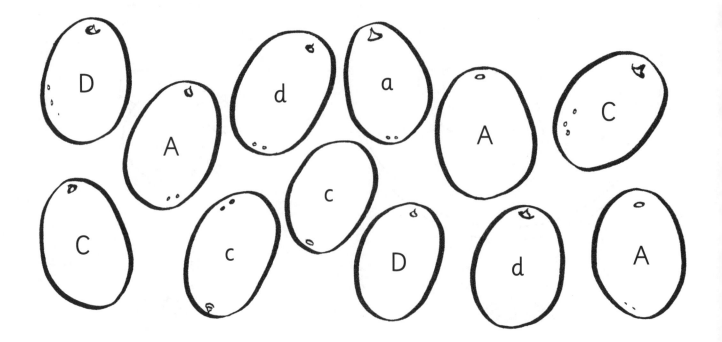

1 Match and colour.

c   d

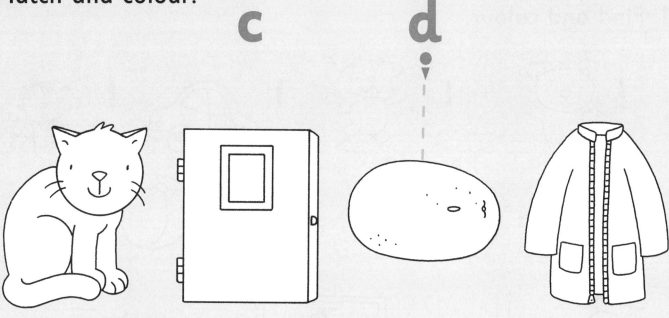

2 Count. Trace the right number.

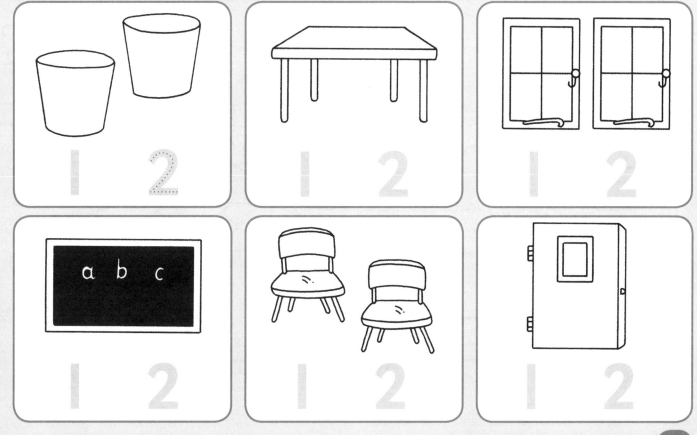

3 My toys

1 Find and colour.

1 Trace the same letter.

a	b	a	c	d
c	a	b	d	c
D	B	A	C	D
B	D	B	A	C

2 Look and say. Circle the letter.

a b c d

a b c d

a b c d

a b c d

1 Trace and write.

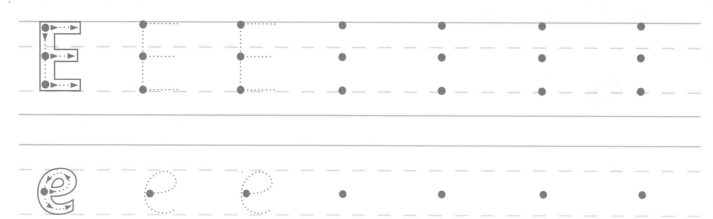

2 Trace and say. Colour.

egg   **e**lephant

1 Draw.

3    4

2 Trace and write.

1 Trace and write.

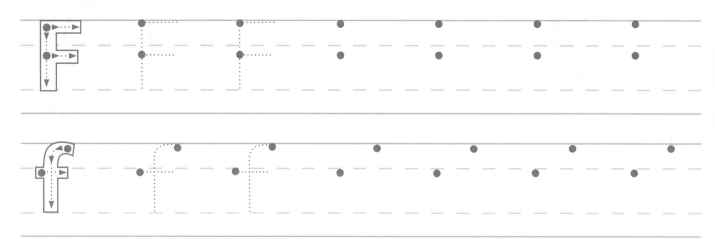

2 Trace and say. Colour.

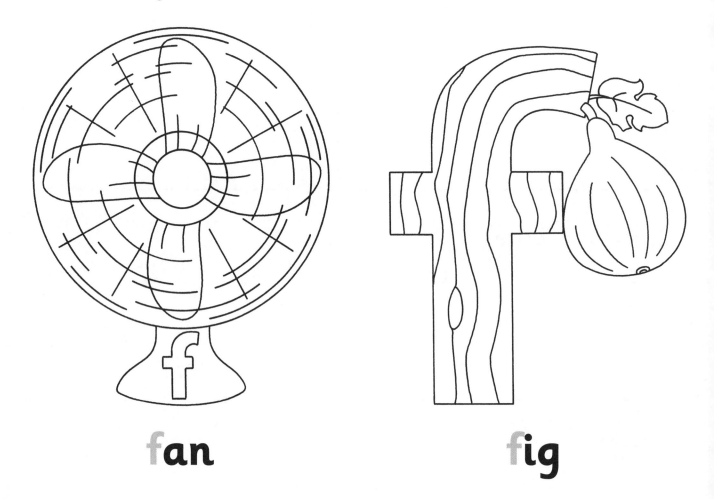

fan   **fig**

1 Colour and say.

1

2

3

4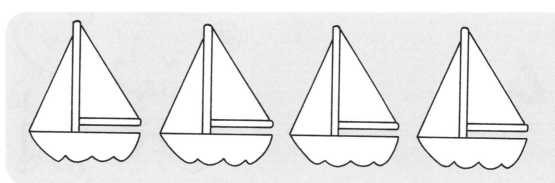

Unit 3 Review

1 Match and colour.

e   f

2 Count and match.

3

4

4 My things

1 Find and circle. Colour.

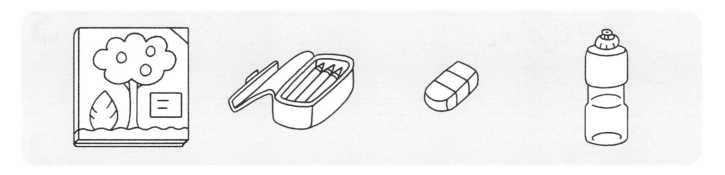

1 Count and match.

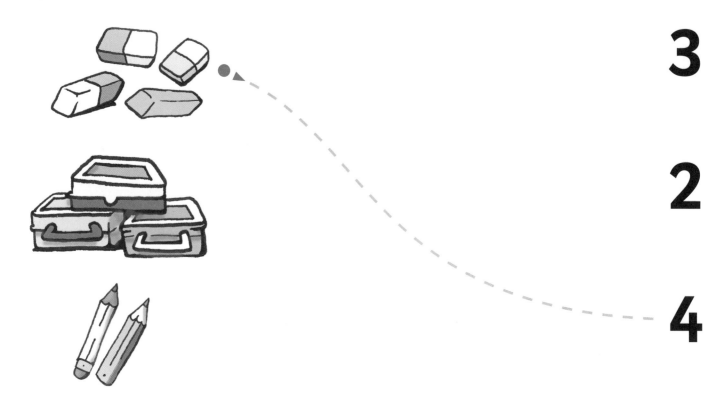

3

2

4

2 Draw, write and say.

4

1 Trace and write.

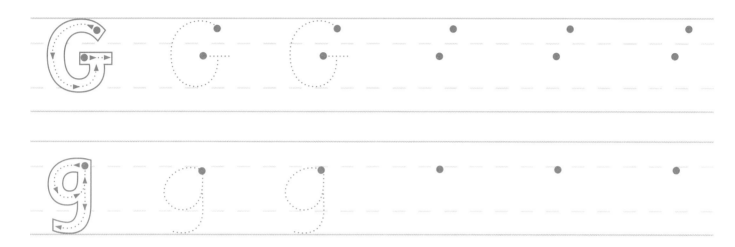

2 Trace and say. Colour.

g**irl**   g**ive**

1 Count, circle and colour.

2 Trace and write.

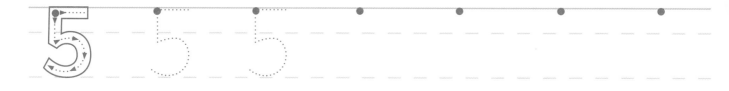

1 Trace and write.

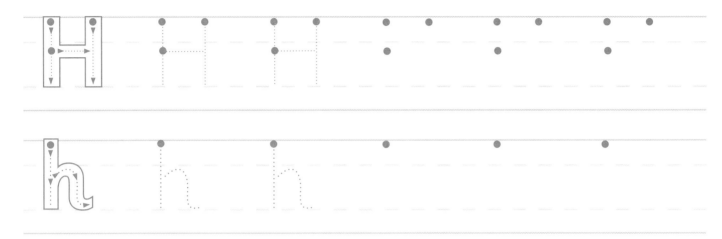

2 Trace and say. Colour.

hand

horse

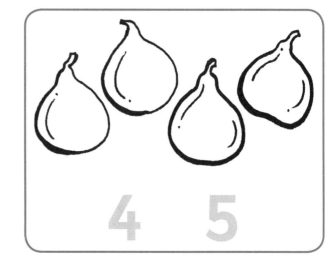

1 Count. Trace the right number.

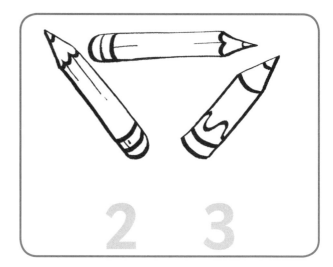

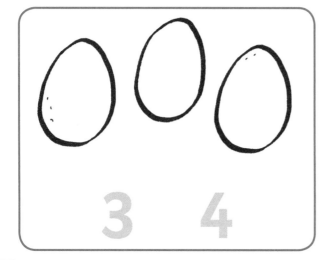

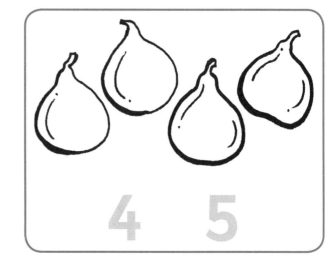

1 Match and colour.

g   h

2 Join the dots. Colour.

Lesson 1

1 Colour.

1 Draw and say.

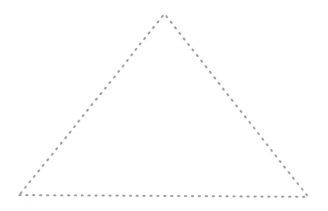

2 Colour.

red   **blue**   **green**   **yellow**

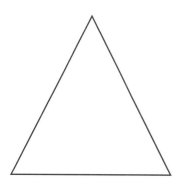

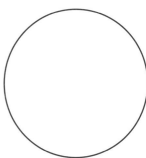

1 Trace and write.

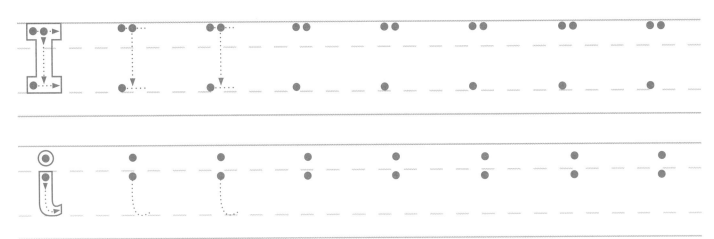

2 Trace and say. Colour.

iguana

insect

1 Count and circle.

2 Trace and write.

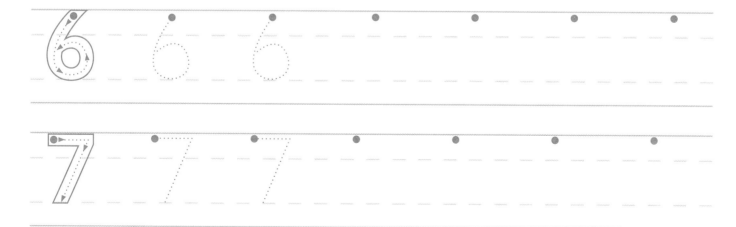

1 Trace and write.

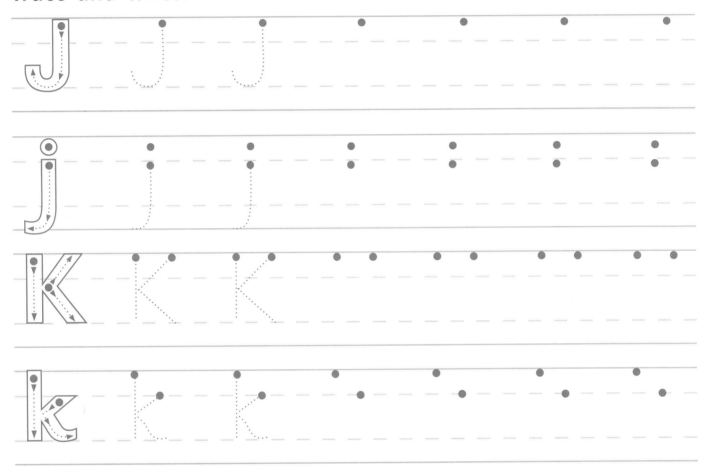

2 Trace and say. Colour.

Jig

jump

kite

1 Match and colour.

red

blue

yellow

green

orange

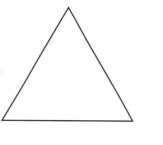

2 Look and say. Circle the letter.

J K I

D B K

H F A

1 Look and say. Trace the letter.

I J K

i j k

i j k

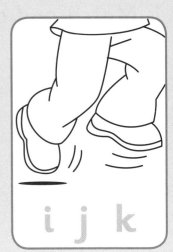
i j k

2 Count and write.

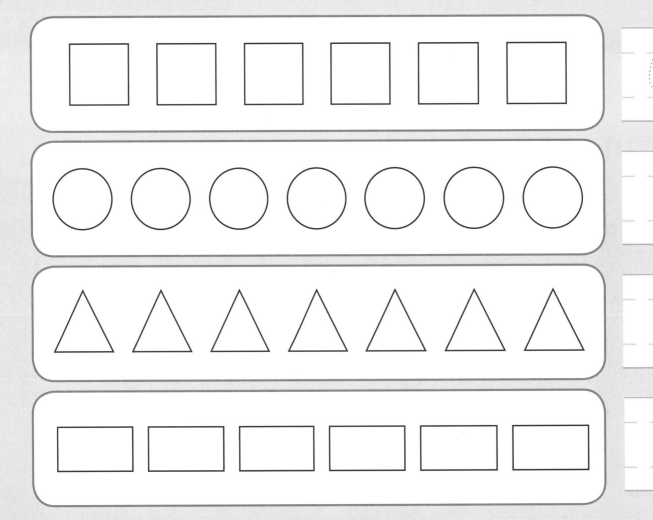

6 My farm

1 Match and colour.

1 Find and colour. Say.

a b c d e f g h i j k

1 Trace and write.

2 Trace and say. Colour.

lion

moon

1 Count and match.

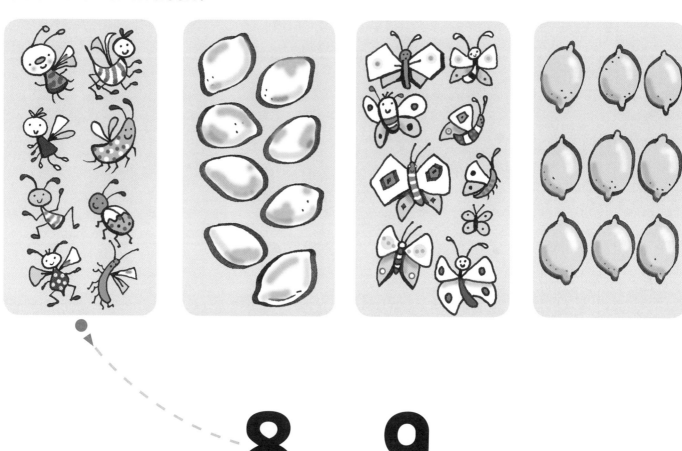

8   9

2 Trace and write.

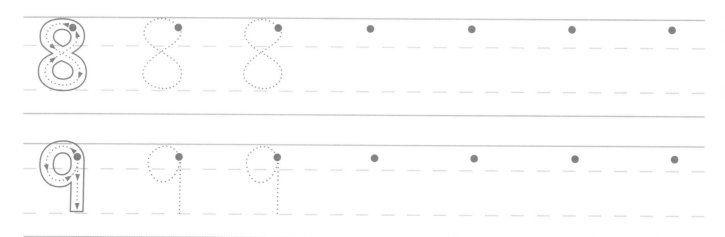

1 Trace and write.

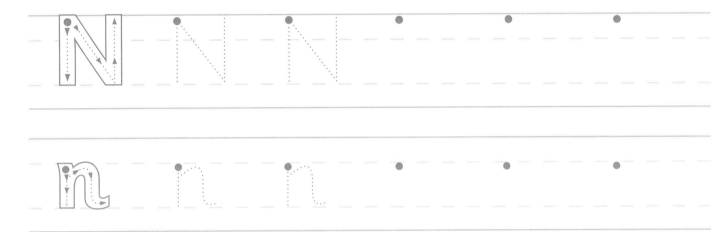

2 Trace and say. Colour.

nose   **n**ut

1 Say and write the letter.

1 Match and colour.

l m n

2 Count and circle.

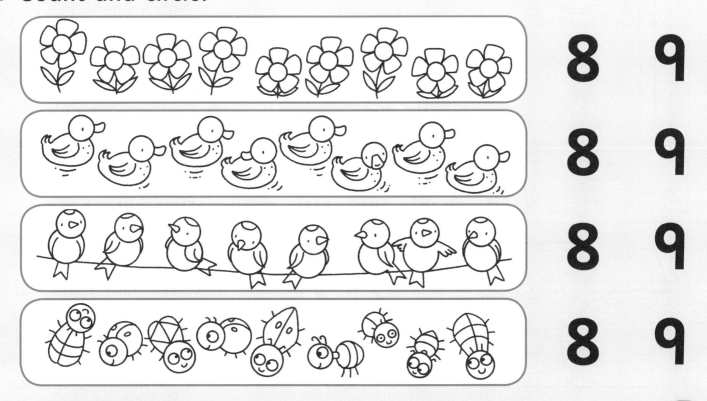

8 9

8 9

8 9

8 9

7 My clothes

1 Find and colour. Say.

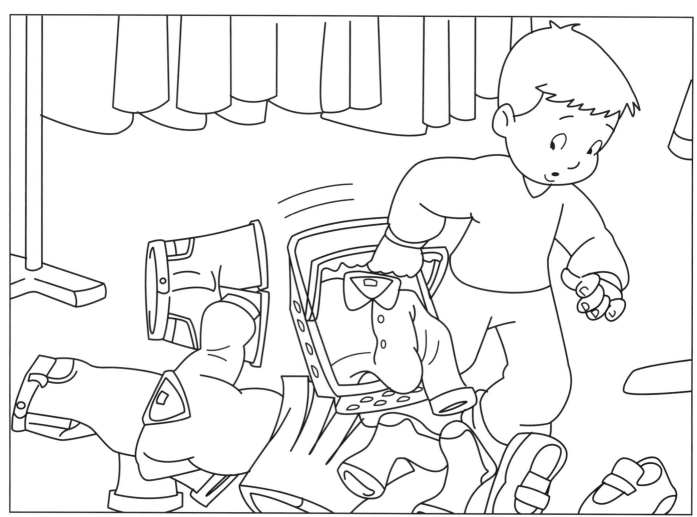

1 Colour.

1 red   2 blue   3 green

4 orange   5 yellow

1 Trace and write.

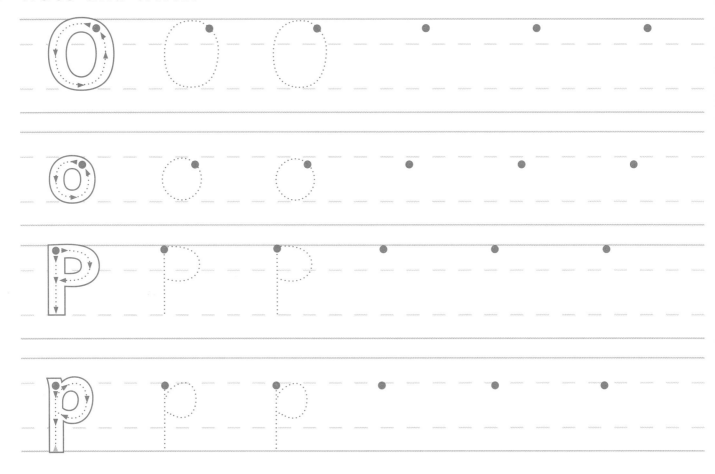

2 Trace and say. Colour.

o**ctopus**

P**at**

p**ink**

1 Trace and write.

2 Count, circle and colour.

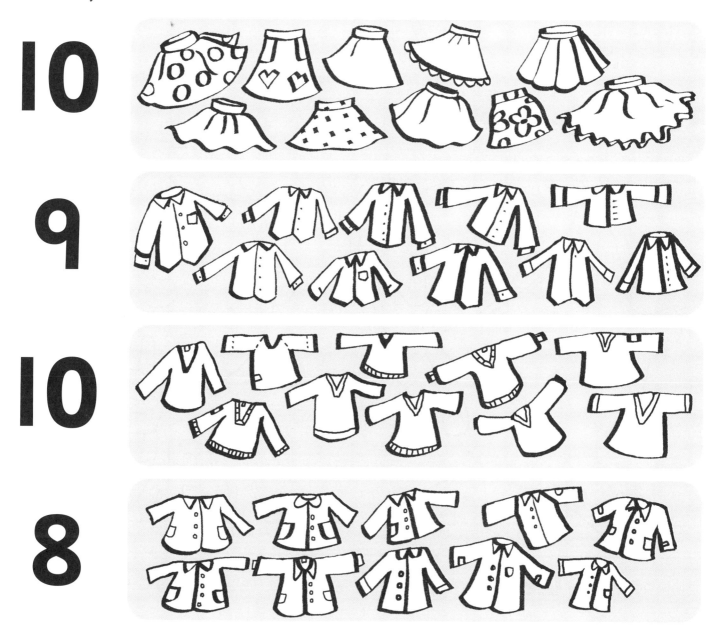

1 Trace and write.

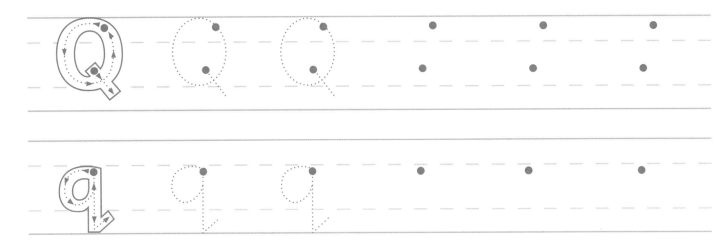

2 Trace and say. Colour.

queen

quiet

1 Join the dots. Colour.

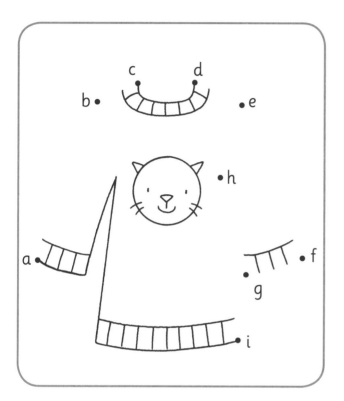

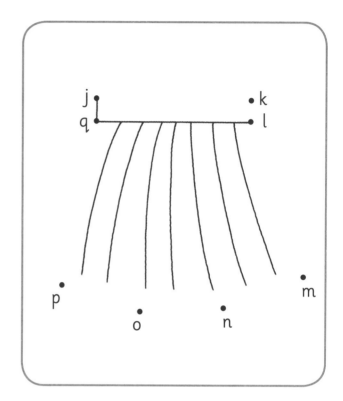

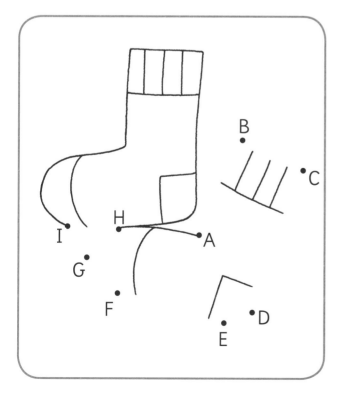

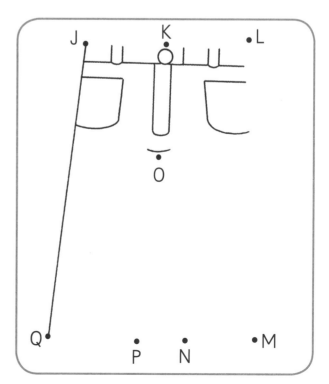

Unit 7 Review

1 Say and write.   **Oo   Pp   Qq**

 ____ at

 ____ ueen

 ____ ctopus

2 Count and write.

8

8 My body

1 Match and colour. Say.

1 Count and write.

2   4   6   8

 8

1 Trace and write.

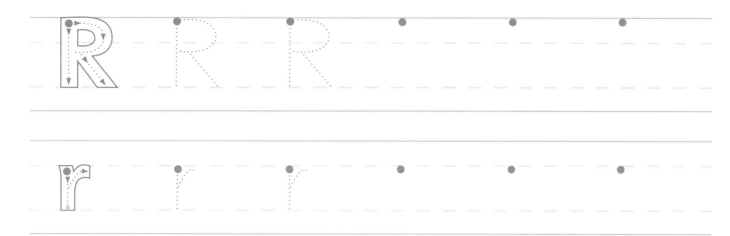

2 Trace and say. Colour.

rabbit

run

1 Draw and colour.

my hand

2 Colour the letters **R** and r.

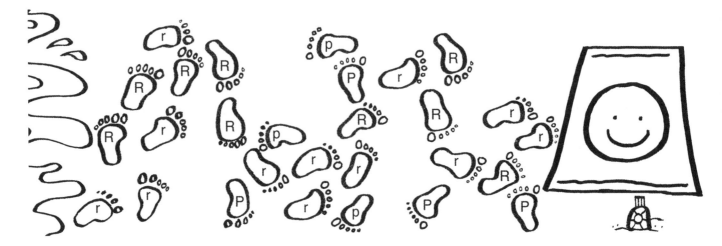

1 Trace and write.

2 Trace and say. Colour.

seesaw

Tess

toes

1 Say and match.

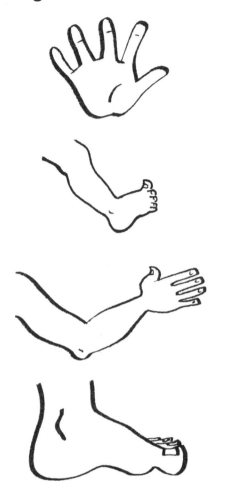

2 Join the dots. Colour.

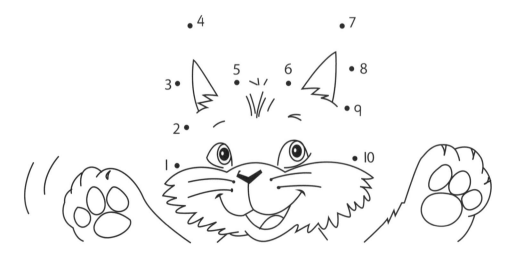

1 Say and write. r s t

____abbit

____un

____ing

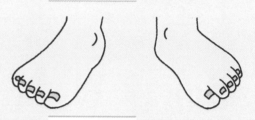

____oes

2 Count and circle.

5 6

2 3

9 8

1 Say and match.

1 Draw and trace.

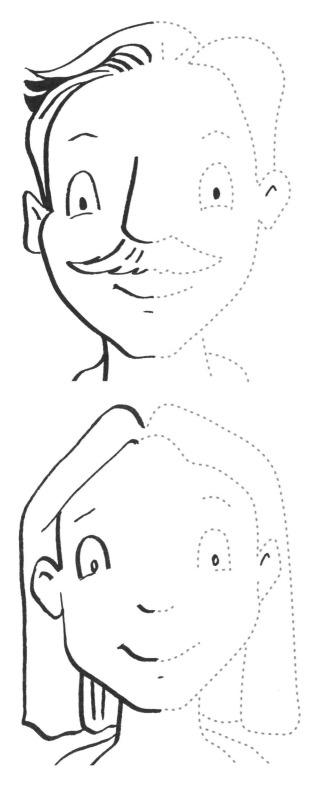

1 Trace and write.

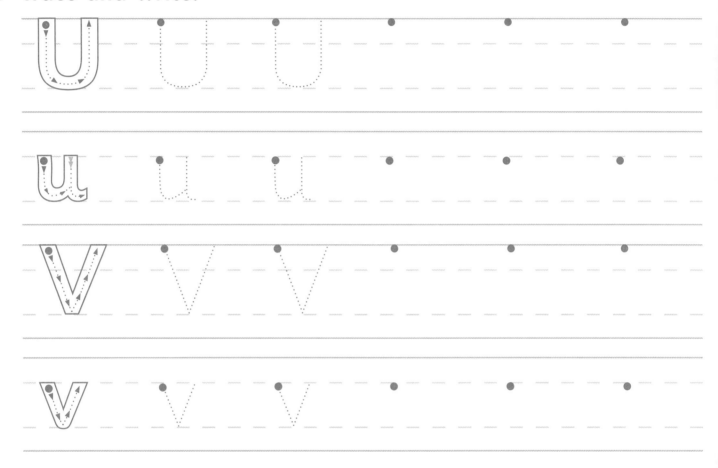

2 Trace and say. Colour.

umbrella

volcano

1 Draw and say.

my family

1 Trace and write.

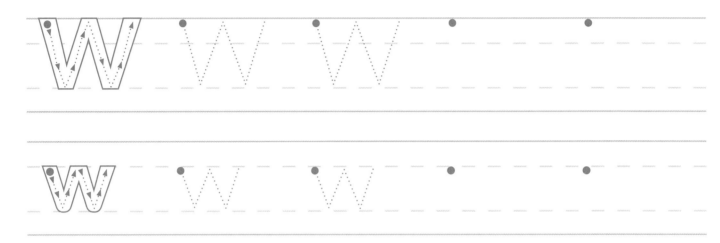

2 Trace and say. Colour.

walk

water

1 Say and match.

1 Find and circle.

v	U	V	W
R	r	P	f
w	V	W	N
Q	p	g	q
u	w	U	v
T	t	f	i

2 Say and write.   u   v   w

  p

  alk

  an

  ater

10 My food

1 Colour.   (1 red ▷ (2 blue ▷ (3 green ▷

(4 orange ▷ (5 pink ▷ (6 yellow ▷

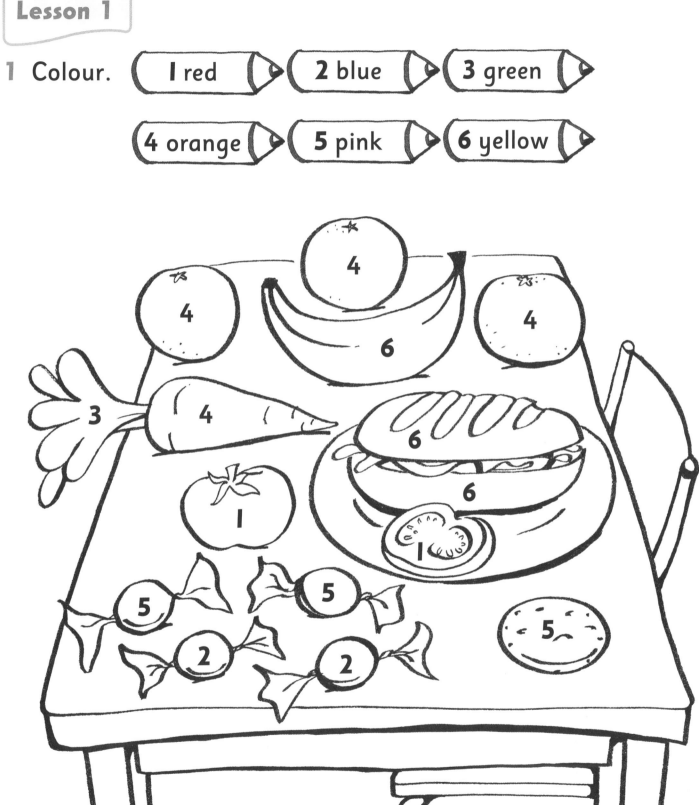

1 Circle and say.

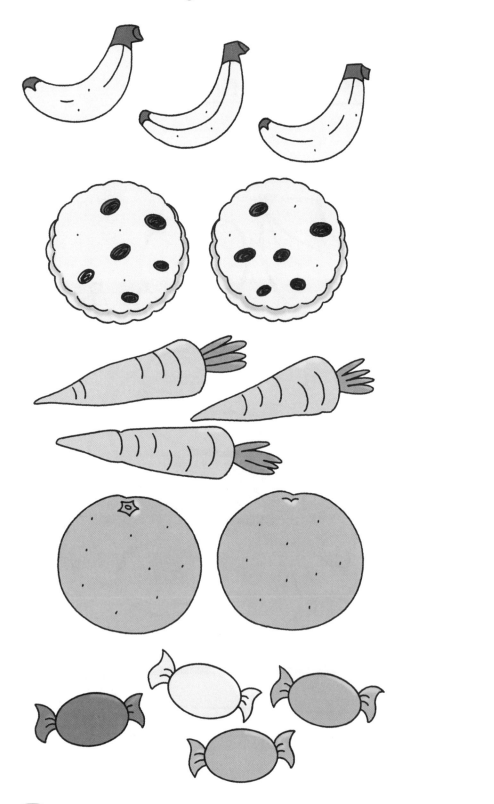

1 Trace and write.

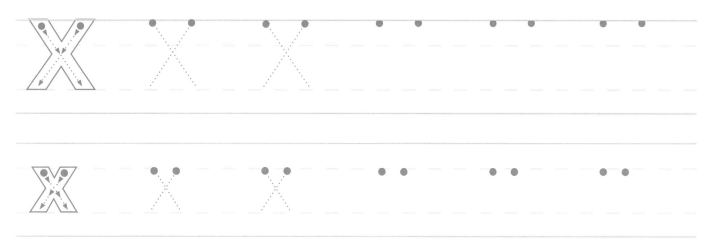

2 Trace and say. Colour.

box   **fox**

Lesson 4

1 Say and write.

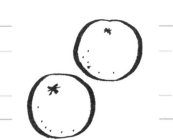

2 Colour the right picture.

1 Trace and write.

2 Trace and say. Colour.

yo-**y**o

zebra

1 Look, count and write.

2 Write and say.

1   2   3   5

     7   9

1 Follow the letters.

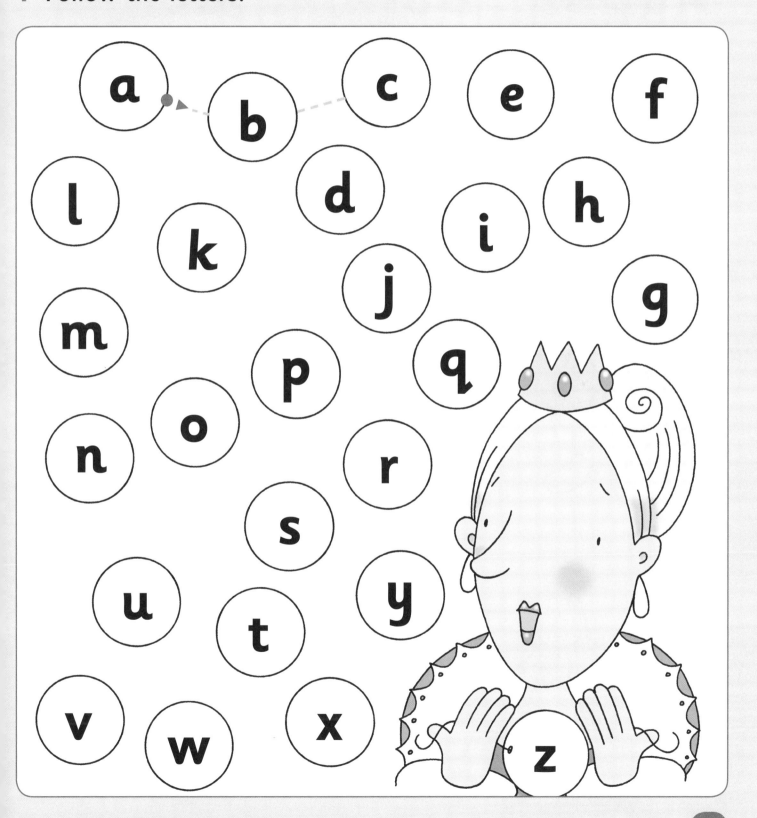

Picture dictionary

A a

B b

C c

D d

E e

F f
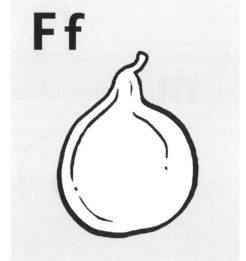

G g

H h
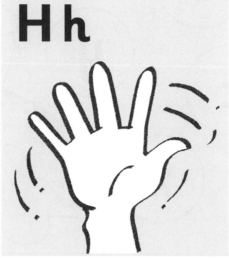

I i

J j

K k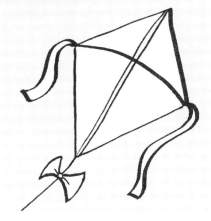

L l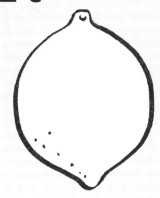

M m

N n

O o

P p

Q q

R r

Picture dictionary

S s

T t

U u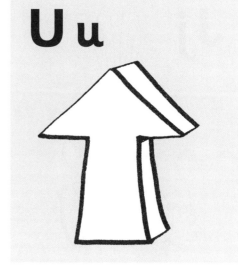

V v

W w

X x

Y y

Z z

Songs

Unit 1

Lesson 2

Hello, Pat!
How are you?

Hello, Jig!
I'm fine, thank you.

Hello, Adam!
How are you?

Hello, Baz!
I'm fine, thank you.

Lesson 4

Point to Jig
Point to Pat
Stand up
Sit down
Clap, clap, clap!

Point to Baz
Point to Tess
Stand up
Sit down
Yes, yes, yes!

Unit 2

Lesson 4

Count one and two
Count one and two
One for me
Two for you

Count one and two
Count one and two
A door for me
A chair for you

Unit 3

Lesson 4

One, two, three, four
Knock, knock,
  knock, on the door
Four, three, two, one
Come in! Time for fun!

Toys for you
Toys for me
Toys, toys, toys
Count with me!

Lesson 6

3, 2, 1
Go, Jig!
Time for fun!

Unit 4

Lesson 2

How old are you?
I'm four.

How old are you?
I'm four.

How old are you?
  How old are you?
I'm four. I'm four. I'm four!

Lesson 4

Doll and teddy bear
Count 1 and 2
Doll and teddy bear
Clap for you

Doll and teddy bear
Count 3 and 4
Doll and teddy bear
Point to the door

Doll and teddy bear
Count to 5

Doll and teddy bear
Ready to hide

1, 2, 3, 4, 5! Hide!

Unit 5

Lesson 4

Look at the iguana.
It's green and blue.
Look at the iguana.
It's hungry, too!

Seven insects flying by.
The iguana looks at the sky.

[Clap]

Six insects flying by.

…

Look at the iguana.
It's green and blue.
Look at the iguana.
It's hungry, too!

One insect flying by.
The iguana looks at the sky.

[Clap]

No insects flying by.

Unit 6

Lesson 4

Listen to the animal,
  animal, animal.
Listen to the animal.
Here is the sound.

Tweet, tweet, tweet, tweet,
  tweet
Tweet, tweet, tweet, tweet,
  tweet
Is it a bird? A bird? A bird?
Yes, it's a bird. Yes, it is.
Tweet, tweet, tweet, tweet,
  tweet
Yes, it's a bird. A bird.
  A bird.

Listen to the animal,
  animal, animal.
Listen to the animal.
Here is the sound.

Meow … [a cat]

Heehaw … [a donkey]

Quack … [a duck]

Unit 7

Lesson 4

Ten birds, here with me
Look at that!
It's a cat!
Fly away, bird! Fly away
  bird!
How many birds here
  with me?
Nine.

…

One bird, here with me
Look at that!
It's a cat!
Go away, cat! Go away, cat!
Come back, birds, come
  back!

Unit 8

Lesson 4

I've got ten fingers
I've got ten toes
I've got two feet
And a little nose

You've got two legs
You've got ten toes
You've got two arms
And a little nose

Unit 9

Lesson 4

Look at my pictures.
This is my family.
Come and meet my family.
Come and meet my family.

She is my mum.
He is my dad.
This is Jig.
And this is Pat.

Adam is my brother.
Baz is my brother.
We are a family.
We love each other.

Unit 10

Lesson 4

A /æ/ U /ʌ/
B /b/ V /v/
C /k/ W /w/
D /d/ X /ks/
E /e/
F /f/
G /g/
H /h/
I /ɪ/
J /dʒ/
K /k/
L /l/
M /m/
N /n/
O /ɒ/
P /p/
Q /kw/
R /r/
S /s/
T /t/

OXFORD
UNIVERSITY PRESS

Great Clarendon Street, Oxford OX2 6DP

Oxford University Press is a department of the University of Oxford.
It furthers the University's objective of excellence in research, scholarship,
and education by publishing worldwide in

Oxford New York

Auckland Cape Town Dar es Salaam Hong Kong Karachi
Kuala Lumpur Madrid Melbourne Mexico City Nairobi
New Delhi Shanghai Taipei Toronto

With offices in

Argentina Austria Brazil Chile Czech Republic France Greece
Guatemala Hungary Italy Japan Poland Portugal Singapore
South Korea Switzerland Thailand Turkey Ukraine Vietnam

OXFORD and OXFORD ENGLISH are registered trade marks of
Oxford University Press in the UK and in certain other countries

ISBN: 978 0 19 443206 1

Printed in China

This book is printed on paper from certified and well-managed sources.

ACKNOWLEDGEMENTS

Illustrations by: Paul Gibbs and John Haslam pp 4, 5, 6, 7, 8, 9, 10, 26 (Adam),
36, 37, 38, 46, 48, 57, 58 (Pat), 60, 65, 74 (Adam, Baz), 75 (Jig, Pat), 76 (Tess), 77,
78; Cathy Hughes pp 5 (fence), 11, 13, 15, 17, 20, 22, 23, 25, 27, 29, 31, 34, 39,
41, 43, 45, 50, 51, 53, 55, 59, 62, 64, 68, 69, 71, 73; Lisa Williams/Sylvie Poggio
Artists Agency pp 12, 14, 16, 18, 19, 21, 24, 26, 28, 30, 32, 35, 40, 42, 44, 47,
49, 52, 54, 56, 58, 61, 63, 66, 67, 70, 72, 74, 75, 76.

oxfordparents
Help your child with English

Visit Oxford Parents for ideas and free activities:
- Advice on developing your child's English skills
- Songs, action games and craft activities
- Video demonstrations

www.oup.com/elt/oxfordparents